First published in Denmark by Gyldendalske Boghandel 1977
First published in Great Britain by Kaye & Ward Ltd
21 New Street, London EC2M 4NT
1977

ISBN 0 7182 1167 7

Printed in Denmark

STIG WEIMAR

Great Britain
is like this

KAYE & WARD · LONDON

Do you know this flag?

It is the Union Jack, the British flag.

In the picture below you can see it flying over the Tower of London. This old fortress was for many years used to imprison Kings, Queens and other noblemen. Today it houses a magnificent armour collection, and the priceless Crown Jewels, used at the Queen's Coronation.

Each country has a different flag. Here, Scouts from
Denmark, Great Britain, Sweden, Africa, USA and several
other nations are gathered.

Each group has hoisted its own flag to show which
country it comes from.

Can you find the tent with the Union Jack?

This is what Great Britain, which is part of the
United Kingdom, looks like. The coloured areas
are land and the white areas are sea. The
northern part, coloured light green,
is Scotland. The dark green part is
England and the blue part is Wales.
On the large yellow island west
of England and Wales, you will
see a small area in the North
coloured green. This is
Northern Ireland. England,
Scotland, Wales and
Northern Ireland
together constitute
the United Kingdom.
Southern Ireland, the yellow
part, does not belong to the
United Kingdom. Southern
Ireland is a country
on its own.

We shall now take a trip round the British Isles and so that you know where we are in the country, on each page there is a small map of Great Britain marked with a red dot. The red dot shows you the place we are talking about.

This picture shows what it looks like in the border country between England and Scotland. In the background you can see the Scottish mountains. The train is on its way from Scotland to England.

The Lake District has the highest mountains and the biggest lakes in England. There are not many roads here and only a few small towns. The countryside is very wild and beautiful.

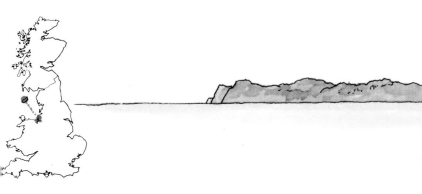

From Liverpool you can easily take the ferry out to the Isle
of Man. During the summer many special events are held
there, the most famous being the thrilling TT Motor Cycle
Races.
The strange thing about the cats on the Isle of Man is that
they are born without a tail – they are called Manx cats.

In the Midlands, north of the city of
Nottingham, is the Sherwood Forest. This area
has great hills and oak trees that are centuries
old. To this day you can see the Major Oak where
Robin Hood, the outlaw who robbed the
rich to give to the poor, is
said to have hidden.

Apart from beautiful countryside in the Midlands, there are many large cities with factories which make everything from cars to aircraft and from china to toys.

The biggest industrial city is Birmingham, the second largest city in England.

DOUBLE DIAMOND

Most people in Wales speak English, but the
Welsh also have a language of their own.
If you go to Anglesey, in North Wales, you can see the
longest place name in Britain. It has fifty-eight letters:

LLANFAIRPWLLGWYNGYLLGOGERYCHWYRNDROBWLLLLANTYSILIOGOGOGOCH

which when translated means "St Marys Church in a
hollow by the white hazel, close to the rapid
whirlpool by the red cave of St Tysilio".

North Wales is an area of great natural beauty.
Here you will find green hills and valleys,
mountains and rivers, and there are also many
beautiful castles to see. The highest mountain in
Wales is Snowdon. In the winter it is covered in
ice and snow, but in the summer you can travel
to the summit in the little mountain train.

In South Wales, north west of the city of Cardiff is the famous Rhondda Valley. Here coal is mined from seams deep under the ground.

Today coal is mainly used to make electricity and we rely on it to heat and light our houses, and to work our radios, television sets, refrigerators and so on.

Cornwall is known for its attractive coastal scenery and many artists go there to paint pictures.

Because of its mild climate, tropical plants and trees grow there. Early daffodils and spring flowers come from Cornwall.

If you travel to Land's End you will see a house with a sign which says "First and Last House in England". Then you know that you can travel no further.

In Devon is the famous Dartmoor – a vast stretch of heather covered moorland of wild beauty and solitude. Everywhere you will see wild ponies and black-faced sheep.

The ponies have been on Dartmoor for hundreds of years and for most of the year they are left to run wild, but they all have owners, and are rounded up each Autumn so that the foals can be branded.

Bournemouth in Hampshire is a favourite holiday resort with seven miles of sandy beaches and a promenade which is free of all traffic. Bournemouth also has a big shopping centre and miles of gardens and parks.

NOTE: Because of boundary changes, Bournemouth is now in Dorset, not Hampshire.

Lord Nelson's old flagship "The Victory" lies in Portsmouth. In command of this ship Lord Nelson led his fleet to many victories against the enemy. Although all this happened more than a hundred years ago, Portsmouth is still one of Britain's chief naval ports.

The stories of Christopher Robin, Winnie the Pooh, and his friends are known to children all over the world.

The man who wrote the Winnie the Pooh stories was A. A. Milne. This is a picture of the house where he lived, Cothford Farm, near the village of Hartfield in Sussex.

If you stand on the white cliffs of Dover and look out over the English Channel, on a clear day you can see the coast of France.

Ships from all over the world sail through the Channel. These vessels fly flags to show which country they come from.

This is Buckingham Palace, in London, where the Queen lives. Every day many people gather outside the palace gates to see the Changing of the Guard.

London is the capital of England and the biggest city in Great Britain. Here, on the banks of the river Thames, are the Houses of Parliament, where the Government make the laws. Big Ben, the famous clock in the 320 ft tower also stands here.

Grimsby is the biggest fishing port in Great Britain. Each day, hundreds of fishing boats sail out to catch fish and often they sail so far away that they are at sea for many days. The catches are auctioned each morning at the dockside, but much of the fish is either smoked or quick frozen and packaged there so that when it reaches your table it is as fresh as if it has just been landed at the quayside.

There are many lakes in Scotland and the largest is Loch Lomond. The longest is Loch Ness, where the legendary Loch Ness Monster is supposed to have been seen. Scientists in submarines and helicopters have long been searching for "Nessie" but to date there is not enough evidence to prove her existence.

Scotland is above all a mountainous country. It has fifty four mountains higher than any in England. Ben Nevis is the highest.

In Aviemore there is a big sports centre where you can ski if weather conditions are right. There is also a skating rink.

In Edinburgh, the capital of Scotland, in the grounds
of the old castle you can see the Scottish soldiers.
The Scots are known all over the world for their
bagpipes and their kilts. The Edinburgh Tattoo is
held here: the colourful military display in which
the various regiments dressed in their own tartans,
march to the sound of the pipes.

Loch Ness

Aviemore

Edinburgh

Gretna Green

The Lake District

Isle of Man

Snowdonia

Sherwood Forest

Grimsby

Birmingham

Cardiff

London

Hartfield

Dove

Dartmoor

Bournemouth

Portsmouth

Land's End

We have now completed our tour of Great
Britain. On the map you can find all the
places we visited during our trip. Of course,
we haven't been to all the interesting places.
That would have taken far too long.
Look at this map, or the map on the back of
the book and see if you can find the place
where *you* live.

The earth on which we live – the whole earth – is like a huge round ball. We call it a sphere. Great Britain lies somewhere on this sphere. The Union Jack shows you where.